A Pilgrim's Guide to Chaos in the Heartland

2005 Concrete Wolf Chapbook Award

Also in the

Concrete Wolf Poetry Chapbook Series

2001

The Grape Painter · Lou Suarez

2002

The Tallahassee Letters · Ryan G. Van Cleave

2003

Such Short Supply · Michelle Brooks

2004

Squeezers · Alison Pelegrin

2005

SPECIAL TWO-CHAPBOOK ISSUE

Put Your Sorry Side Out · Lois Marie Harrod

The Way Out West · J.R. Thelin

A Pilgrim's Guide to Chaos in the Heartland

∞ *Poems* ∞

JESSICA GOODFELLOW

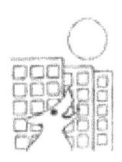

Concrete Wolf Chapbook Series

Concrete Wolf Chapbook Series

ISBN 0-9717671-9-X

Printed in The United States of America

Designed and composed in 11.3/14.3 Fournier MT with
FF Meta display at Hobblebush Books, Brookline, NH
(www.hobblebush.com).

ABOUT THE COVER ILLUSTRATION:

The Flammarion woodcut is an enigmatic woodcut by an unknown artist. It is referred to as the "Flammarion woodcut" because its first documented appearance is in Camille Flammarion's *L'atmosphère: mètèrologie populaire* (*The Atmosphere: Popular Meteorology*, Paris, 1888). The woodcut was widely circulated at the end of the 19th century, when it was commonly assumed that people from the Middle Ages believed the earth was flat. Today professional medievalists agree that this notion of a "medieval flat earth" was a misconception.

—Excerpted from Wikipedia, en.wikipedia.org/wiki/Flammarion_woodcut

Published by:

Concrete Wolf
PO Box 1808
Kingston, WA 98346

www.ConcreteWolf.com

ConcreteWolfPress@gmail.com

for my grandmother, Beth Christensen Taylor

and, in memory of my grandfather, Perry Young Taylor

Acknowledgments

Grateful acknowledgement is made to the following journals for publishing my poems:

5 AM: "How to Recognize Your Own Shadow"
Beloit Poetry Journal: "A Pilgrim's Guide to Chaos in the Heartland"
DIAGRAM: "Lagrange's Problem"
Isotope, A Journal of Literary Nature and Science Writing: "Navigating by the Light of a Minor Planet," under the title "Ephemerides of a Minor Planet"
Parnassus Literary Review: "The Difference Between Doing and Being"
Phoebe: A Journal of Literature and Art: "Imagine No Apples" and "Spatial Relations"
RATTLE: "The Beach at Big Salt"

My sincere thanks to the following people for their suggestions and encouragement in the preparation of these poems: Lana Hechtman Ayers, Mary Bast, Shannon Borg, Lydia Dishman, Jeannine Hall Gailey, E. Bruce Hoch, Kerry Hudson, Mia Kammeyer-Mueller, Christy Sanford, Suzanne Schwertley, Abe Spevack, Jennifer Srygley, Eldon Turner, Peggy Wolfson, Shellie Zacharia, and all the Gainesville Poets and Writers.

Grateful acknowledgement of financial and moral support received from the Emrys Foundation in the form of the Dr. Linda Julian Essay Award, and from the Beloit Poetry Journal in the form of the Chad Walsh Poetry Prize.

Gratitude to the following people for their unswerving love and support: Jacki Donaldson, Leslie James, JaNee Goodfellow Russon, Anne Wickboldt, and Rutecleia Zarin.

Special thanks to: Beth Taylor, Shoko Ueno, and the Goodfellow family. And of course, all thanks and love to my husband and sons, Naohiko, Taiyo and Hugo Ueno.

Contents

A Pilgrim's Guide to Chaos in the Heartland

Imagine No Apples

All beginnings wear their endings like dark shadows.
—Chet Raymo, astronomer-physicist

All beginnings wear their endings like dark apples.
A is for apple. B is not for apple.
C, also not for apple. And so on.
Everything always ends up apple, or not apple.
Pick any beginning and there's the apple,
never falling far enough from the tree:
the apple and the omega.

All beginnings wear their apples like dark shadows.
For example, Eve in the Garden
stood beneath the Tree of Knowledge,
biting into forbidden fruit.
Beguiled but enlightened, sated and falling
she dragged all humanity with her by bruised heels—
suddenly everyone banished from paradise.

All apples wear their shadows like dark endings.
For example, Newton in the garden
dozed beneath a tree, dreamt of seeking knowledge,
awoke to see a red globe falling.
Drowsy but enlightened with heaviness,
he saw one sad secret of the universe revealed—
suddenly everyone stuck to this planet.

All dark shadows wear their endings like beginnings.
But suppose not. Imagine no apples:

everyone still naked; all of physics stymied.
No one to say, "Oh, this is gravity,"
or "Ah, this is sin."
Would we be better off, would we be happier,
sinless and floating, or if not actually floating,
still capable of hoping to rise.

The Mother of Nations Waits

Sarai, the Baroness of Barrenness,
the woman with a womb like a memory like a sieve,
sent a valentine to Wittgenstein, a poem to Plotinus,
a letter to Leibniz, inventor of the binary code.
Across the bottom of the pages, in lieu of *X's* and *O's*,
she scrawled strings of ones and zeros,
promises of everything and nothing,
and nothing in between.
(Not one answered.)

In the time before zeros
merchants marked nothing with nothing,
leaving spaces to show where something was missing.
But what shape was the space?
Sarai wanted to know, pressing on her midriff,
hoping that containing the emptiness
was a possibility.

And then there were zeros, just like that!
From Babylon came symbols whose presence
meant the absence of everything else.
All losses were made equal,
which was a relief to Sarai
and which wasn't.

Later Leibniz would spin whole worlds
out of ones and zeros
but what can you make from only zeros?
Whatever you add, that's still all you've got
and maybe you've lost yourself for the effort.
You can't be a little bit pregnant.

Abraham called to Sarai, husband of her broken heart,
but she was bent over a mathematics text,
muttering in not-yet-invented codes
(zeros and ones, eggs and sperm)
and she didn't hear.

Isaac called to her, son of her broken womb,
and she could not hear; an angel and a ram rescued him instead.
Or she heard, but could not believe she had heard.
Because while the opposite of being fertile is being barren,
the opposite of being barren is still being barren.

Lagrange's Problem

By his fifth decade Lagrange no longer
reckoned celestial mechanics.
Already he'd wrestled the moon's libration,
why it veils but one face to show earth,
and "The Problem of Three Bodies,"
the lover's triangle on which teeters
the earth, moon and sun.

Lagrange courted equations, shunned intuition.
The slip of liquids, the shove of solids
he would not differentiate
choosing the dry elegance of algebra
over the earth's crude beauty.
Fluxion he distrusted;
only finite quantities spoke to him.
In his version of the calculus
the concept of vanishing vanished,
till there remained nowhere to hide.
Lagrange put down his pen.

Renouncing his efforts to quantify the night,
Lagrange edged into unknown variables.
All of France mourned. Marie Herself Antoinette
couldn't compel the sad genius to calculate.
The planets were no more and no less
perturbed in the slide of their orbits.

Of knowing, there is no end.
Or, there is an end.
One curse and its opposite,
also a curse.
Reasons to pray are the same
as reasons to forsake praying.

Happily the war summoned Lagrange,
duty over disgust.
For the first time in years
from his vast empty desk
he lifted his head and from his left ear
out tumbled *le système métrique*.
Thus the earth's disinherited
could measure, at last, their losses
in tenths, and tens, and powers of ten.

The Invention of Fractions

God himself made the whole numbers: everything else is the work of man.
—Leopold Kronnecker

God created the whole numbers:
the firstborn, the seventh seal,
Ten Commandments etched in stone,
the Twelve Tribes of Israel –
Ten we've already lost –
forty days and forty nights,
Saul's ten thousand and David's ten thousand.
'Be of one heart and one mind' –
the whole numbers, the counting numbers.

It took humankind to need less than this;
to invent fractions, percentages, decimals.
Only humankind could need the concepts
of splintering and dividing,
of things lost or broken,
of settling for the part instead of the whole.

Only humankind could find the whole numbers,
infinite as they are, to be wanting;
though given a limitless supply,
we still had no way
to measure what we keep
in our many-chambered hearts.

A Pilgrim's Guide to Chaos in the Heartland:

1. Road Trip

It's a good idea to collect as much entropy
as possible before using a system.
—Jon Callas, cryptographer

Because the horizon is not a number line,
because distance is an absolute value,
I use the atlas as an *I Ching*, a rune,
my calculations point to the Midwest,
as good a place as any.

Here in the disappe5aring prairie
I finally understand
how some infinities can be larger,
others smaller; how certain endless
quantities move closer to no end
faster than others.
Aleph Null—countable though infinite:
grass, sun, treelessness.
Aleph One—uncountable and infinite:
dust, wind, fire. The distance
between here and God.

And this I did not expect,
that the lon7eliness would be countable.

My son wants a tumbleweed for a pet,
now one is buckled in the back seat.
What a clever boy, choosing to love
a thing already dead and rootless.

At the motel, he watches me
lower the blinds against
the white noise, the presence
of all possibilit5ies in the night.
"It's such a lovely dark, Mama," he says.

2. Devices of Chance

Definition of Randomness: an inexplicable misfeature; gratuitous inelegance.

—WWW.GOPHER.QUUX.ORG:70

Two Defi4nitions of Randomness, Each Necessary but Not Sufficient:

Numbers in a string are random if they cannot be expressed in an2y shorter form.

But that is just poetry.

Numbers in a sequence are random if there is no patte6rn to them.

Is that unbel5ief or its absence?

Ways to Generate Randomness/Pseudorandomness:

throwi2ng dice, casting lots, flipping coins, d9rawing balls from hoppers, drawing straws, picking num0bers from 1 to *x*, playing rock/paper/scissors, consulting random number tables, spooling algor9ithms through computers

getting out of bed in the morni7ng

A Short History of Dev7ices of Chance:

Casting lots (ancient beyond history): object1s, cast to the earth, or into a recepta0cle and then drawn out—pebbles or die, nuts or barleycorn, tw9igs, bones, coins, cards, yarrow sticks, precious gems. Once believed to reveal the will of god(s).

D3ice (circa 2750 B.C., ancient Mesopotamia/the Indus Valley): fashioned from clay and passed through fire, dotted with pips mu8ch as today's.

The astralagus (earlier than 1320 B.C., Egypt): dice-like bones with four fac9es, each different in shape.

The quincunx (1823-4, Sir Francis Dalton, cousin to Darwin): the theory of errors m3odelled by pellets, dropped through a vertical maze of pins, landing in a bell shape that echoes the no9rmal curve.

The ancients, too, wanted to live as though there wasn't enou1gh randomness in life, as if it had to be sought out like a buried fam3ily secret, or something feral; as though it wouldn't come looking for you in the night.

These days we know the sources of pure randomness are few. We measu5re cosmic ray flux, light emiss4ions from trapped mercury molecules, thermal noise from resistors, the decay of radioacti8ve material.

Trapped. Re9sist. Decay.

3. Grassla6nds

And Aaron shall cast lots upon the two goats;
one lot for the Lord, and the other lot for the
scapegoat. . . . And the goat shall bear upon him
all their iniquities unto a land not inhabited:
and he shall let go the goat in the wilderness.
—LEVITICUS 16: 8, 22

We haven't pass7ed another car all day,
j6ust the grasses undulating,
the winds ululating,
oceans of air drow749ning us.
In every dir7ection
the startling sameness—
easy to get lo3st,
imp4ossible to be lost.

Here in the New W4orld
eve8ryone wanders.
39787637
Fold the nation in half
le9ngthwise, endwise,
and the intersectio1n,
the pivot point, the spot
wher4e the map would crack fi3rst,
dead center, bla9ck hole,
is not far from here. 0

Perha6ps from that spot, south76westerly,
a tornado is h2eaded this way—
a conic7al tumbl3eweed,
a vortex, an altar,
a lot cast65 on the plains

5touching down here, ta9king
this one, leaving that one.
The sky turns briefly gre07en,
e9xplodes with missi9ves of ice,
the soun9d of ten thous58and waterfalls,
white noise, maskin7g our sounds,
chaff in the whirlwind40440.

Enter pure ran11domness:
708015impossible to be
lost; where pointle7ssness
is the po36int.

4. C7ounting Backwards

White noise frequently isn't.

—JON CALLAS, cryptographer

05181261

The Tall08 Grass P5rairie States:

Nebraska, th0e Dakotas, Oklahom3a, Texas, Wisco5nsin, Missouri, Kans1as . . . Staring at the para6llel rows of parallel 01 cornstalks, I remember that over h14alf of all Americans liv7e in the State in which they were born640.

Behi3nd me, my son begins co8unting backwards.

Co2mmon Uses for Counting Bac36kwards: 9684996263

to test for a6ging-related declines, dyslexi6a, and, in Texas, drunk dr3iving; to increase concentrat4ion, to fa9ll asleep, in
901272 meditation; to hei8ghten anticipation, as in annou9ncing beauty pageant winner8s or rocket launches

to connect w7ho you are with where you are

176833

How to Dis6tinguish a Child from 6an Adult:

For a child, countin06g backwards is as easy as counting for76ward9s. An adult says5, "Anythi3ng could happen," but is surpr7ised when it does. Or doesn't; the future as 8unsure as the past. 7173Co4unting backwards is impossible: betw10een any two number4s there are infinitely 07many more. 097

Counting forwards is worse.

How to Tell if You Are A M32athematician:

If you thin2k rand7omness is desirable and too rar5e, like rubies; if you chase6 8entropy, like a butter33fly once thought to be extinc50t, you are a 036434 mathematic8ian.7652

86357

If you think r4andomness is as ubiq01uitous and welcome as dust, t3he common cold, tract housin5g; if you would run9 from entrop8y if only there were an6ywhere to run, you are no34t a mathematician.

Over half of all America6ns are not mathematicians.

73548768095909

1173929274

1705

5. Crop Circles5

There are several ways not to walk in the prairie,
and one of them is with your eye on a far goal . . .
—William Least Heat Moon

Left, r9ight, straight—
each cros5sroad seems mome9ntous
yet insignificant. I 69572
have lon4g since lost
3360699 the at5las, let go fistfu3ls
of yarrow sticks7 out the wi6ndow
of the8 rental car, like dan54delion
dander in the dry w2ind, cosmic 5116877121
03101ray flux, lig04ht
radiating from som8ething trap6ped.
128

I am c8oming to the Am3erican m44id-
point, the 056epicenter,
0111668014groun9d zero, the cal4m 76867
8at the eye of the s94torm.
Colle8cting entropy 155as I go.

Nowh7ere I have ever been 0100
is any different fro6m 2here. 5023760
The buffa4lo grass and wild bergamot,
spiderwort la83sting only a day0858—
the 03prairie could be a latticed cit8y,
2962 ragged mou2ntain, roofless de4sert, or 04020082
what it is.

I am b5ecoming th8e center of some circ5le,
all p9oints equi05distant from72 me,
interc2hangeable. I a2m zero-
ing in on random355ness.

4037206361 2916650842268953

533476435080

My so4n has said noth19ing
for fi3fty-three miles3.
In the re6arview mirr792or
I see him asle533ep,
his f3ace pressed 4into the tumb5leweed
09303232090256O159
I will have to soo7n let go
019like a scapegoat in the wil4derness.

2428426290833 68353

6. 015Random N6umber Tab8le

We know what randomness
isn't, not what it is.
—William A. Dembski

813398851119929170310601080545571824063530342614867990743923
403097328526977602020516569268665748187305385247186238857963

The Beach at Big Salt

Tools of antiquity—the compass, the straight edge—
could not square the circle, couldn't tame
its numberless sides. Arcs, curves, chords
of circles remain, tracing hollows of shells,
clawed waves, parabolas of sand. See
how matter curves around the emptiness,
how it cups and gently holds
the space where things are absent.
Matter buckles and spirals around it,
proving what is missing is more potent
than what isn't.

Matter aches to escape the discipline of being.
Creation longs to possess the freedom
from being a thing begotten. Even babies
in their mothers' wombs lie curled,
crouched around the swell of the primordial.
Straight or curved, tools cannot measure
what it means to be, after all this time,
still nascent, beholden to what
you can never know.
Armless, legless, a seahorse
unrolls his tail, reels it in endlessly
bobbing and straining in the tides.

Navigating by the Light of a Minor Planet

The trouble with belief in endlessness is
it requires a belief in beginninglessness.
Consider friction, entropy, perpetual motion.

And the trouble with holding to both is that
belief in endlessness requires a certain hope
while belief in beginninglessness ends in the absence of hope.

Or maybe it's vice versa. Luckily,
belief in a thing is not the thing itself.
We can have the concept of origin, but no origin.

Here we are then: in a world where logic doesn't function,
or else emotions can't be trusted. Maybe both.
All known tools of navigation require an origin.

Otherwise, there is only endless relativity and then
what's the point of navigation, in a space where
it's hard to be lost, and even harder not to be?

Saying "I don't want to be here," is not the same
as saying "I want to not be here." It rains
and it rains and it rains the things I haven't said.

The Exchange

Walk among the mangroves
where spiny roots have the bowed heads
and sloping shoulders of knobby Madonnas.
Some clutch tiny Messiahs;
most are empty-handed,
guiltily exchanging light for ground.
I have squandered my squatter's rights
on gravity; now there is no escaping it.

Beatitudes for the earthbound,
the not quite contrite of spirit,
the unbroken of heart:
Those who fear the future
feel superior to those who don't.
Those who want the impossible
pity the easily satisfied.
Those who believe in forever
are, paradoxically, impatient
with those who don't.
Do the ones who see angels in the shadows know
that even water has a shadow?
In winter, even breath?
Do haloes support the wave theory
or the particle theory of light?

But those who've learned to submit
bear the hardest task:
Never quite choosing between
the god that transcends suffering
and the one who embraces it.

Advanced Alchemy

Somehow down the ages
Alchemy got a bad name,
claiming everything is spun
from one primal matter
more elemental than fistfuls of dirt
studded with pill bugs, pelleting
their tiered bodies against change.

Now it's called Superstring Theory,
parts more perfect than the whole.
Because relativity and quantum mechanics
can't both be right.
Because particle theory only works
when we pretend gravity doesn't exist
which only children can do
with both elegance and aplomb,
their bodies airborne as electrons.

Today my younger son asked,
"Which do you like better,
the letter Q or a fish?"
Even the smallest cannot resist
the innate and ancient urge
to spin gold out of everything,
to seek The Mother of All Theories,
a one-size-fits-all god,
atonement on the house.

There are truths divine
to seek but disastrous to find,

facts more afraid of us
than we are of them,
wisdom feral and raw.
Some nights the universe hums a tune
and we do not know the words.
Some of us sing along anyway.
"Q   Q   Q," we chirp.
Murmur, "Fish   fish   fish."

Note: The Italicized lines in the second stanza are borrowed from Brian Greene, and from www.superstringtheory.com.

True North

Day follows night. Night follows day.
Myopic as lovers, they walk hand-in-hand.
Lonely is the nomad who dwells with them.

It is December for the first time in years.
You awaken to no sound, a choir of hermits
not chanting outside your tent flap.

Repeat after the wind: Nothing
unusual can happen to me.
As long as your shadow tattoos the ground,

believe it. The moon is talking
to herself again. Repeat after the moon:
Nothing usual can happen to me.

You must ride chaos bareback and backwards.
You must scale the latitudes
as if they were stars. Remember

a map and a mirror, the photograph
of your twinless twin. Remember
Bergman's Rule: the farther north,

the larger the mammals.

In Praise of Imperfect Love

Courtesans of tenth century Japan knew
the keening of the caged copper pheasant,
solo double-note aria for a missing mate,
could be silenced with a mirror.

The ideal of a love that completes
masks a yearning for homeostasis,
a second umbilical, island fever,
harmony tighter than unison—

dull as a solved equation;
like the ex-lover who said,
"Being with you is like being alone."
He meant it as a compliment.

Spatial Relations

If space exists, it must be contained in something . . . more space, and so on indefinitely. . . . Zeno concludes that there is no space. . . . a denial of the view that space is an empty container. Thus . . . we must not distinguish between a body and the space in which it is.

—Bertrand Russell

In college calculus I learned
of a family of curves—
each, when rotated about an axis,
traces shells of finite volume
but infinite surface area.
"You can fill it with paint,
but can't paint it," said the professor.
"You can drink the bottomless
wine flask dry."

Tonight I am convinced there is endless
space, and you in it somewhere.
Since you've gone, even time is space.
What were my fingertips tracing,
nothing
next to nothing?
While your hands hovered
over everyone.
Always asymptotic, reaching
but not touching. Filling
but not covering, not comforting.

Somewhere someone tonight is rotated
on an axis, and set down, filled,
next to you. Sleeping,
she dreams of abandoned journeys,

uncrossable borders, barriers, boundaries.
And you looking over
the curve of her shoulder.

Infinite regress.
Space containing space containing
space; yet nowhere
to escape this endless envelope
leaking, always, space.

Infinite regrets.
Tonight I understand why
you were trying to learn,
like Zeno of Elea, not
to distinguish between a body
and the space in which it is.

How to Recognize Your Own Shadow

My husband and I agree
on almost nothing. I told him
I would write this
in a poem. He said
I shouldn't.
Which was the correct response.

living in the pond out our window co-existing there are three turtles two this morning on the narrow north end one on the longer east bank all three are sunning are basking but no now one northern turtle has backed into the pond submerging himself among the murkiness shortly he reappears on the east shore and the basking continues all morning he ferries himself between the other two and I imagine them each calling to him *no one is more absent from me than you* and the submerged one answers and *no one from me more than me* but late afternoon I see four turtles on the east bank and none on the north and all are about the same size and now I can't tell which is who has been where all day and now I don't know

People wonder why we stay
together. Only with myself
do I disagree more than I do
with him. I think the same
is true for my husband.
He says *It isn't.*

The Difference Between Doing and Being

We've had this argument before—
you go off to your temple
and the dead that need consoling.
I want to know *why*
the dead need us to be consoling,
and not the other way around.
Also, why do they need consoling
and not consolation?

You say I have never understood
those things that have no centers.

Strategy of Change

For someone who hates change, or claims to,
she has wrestled with the Angel of Chaos once too often.
Though she leaves her menorah up through April,
mornings when she opens her closet, out fall hundreds of personas.
For the people who love her, this is tiresome, as well as tiring.
But she pretends not to notice. Or doesn't notice.

Once she told me she's the most consistent person she knows.
I counted five careers and seven lovers in just the past three years,
and four changes of address and one religious dalliance;
also several shades of hair and a pair of colored lenses.
When I added them up for her, she looked at me, startled.
"That's just what I mean," she said. "Exactly what I'm saying."

If she could, she'd give mathematics back to the ancient Greeks,
who had no zero, no notion of nothingness, no empty sets.
She'd rearrange your memories and make them all seem
equally poignant, as if each had happened only yesterday.
She'd make new names for all the colors, and new colors,
and the words would all be songs, but songs without words.

She can do none of this. Instead, when possible she ignores the rules,
going solo to the places normally peopled by groups,
yet dragging you along through sad embarrassing intimacies.
She reaches into herself and whatever it is she finds there, she flings
upon the world. She empties herself out, then starts again. Yet,
she hates change. Change is the failure to find what she's looking for.

Having no method of invention but the process of elimination—
unorganized and random—if you were to say all her efforts
amounted to nothing, she'd not find it surprising. This does not

deter her; she doesn't believe in entropy, continues her ceaseless
creating. Even she is too realistic to hope to remake the world.
So she starts with herself. She is looking for a counterexample;

trying to refute the given that the empty set is a subset
of all sets; that all sets contain the empty set. Failing that,
she wants to *be* the empty set. She is making plans to become god.
Warned all could implode, she says she'll take her chances.
"Chances to changes is a single downward stroke." "Of the pen?"
"That too." She is laughing as she says this; she is weeping.

She, who hates change, understands that even chaos is better
than the alternative. Assuming, of course, there's a difference.
Assuming, of course, there is an alternative.
We, who learned in school and in other places as she did,
that nature abhors a vacuum, don't even assume angels
but stand back and watch her wrestling nothing.

About the Author

Jessica Goodfellow has a Master's degree in Social Science from the California Institute of Technology, and has worked as a university math teacher, financial analyst, English teacher, and editor. Recipient of the Chad Walsh Poetry Prize, she has work appearing in Best New Poets 2006 and various journals including the *Beloit Poetry Journal*, *Isotope*, and *RATTLE*. She grew up in Philadelphia, Pennsylvania, and now lives in Kobe, Japan, with her husband and two sons. This is her first chapbook.

5497879845432424144978756544949345646511894984984546115214328949847
1915135547742256466516513215641414464621730316456476573723023246361615
6565476898167835891567491568956175685845225675552493417919961473474
8152101534754251291321234564506651236712472791427199745719718211987
7914791447514714719421947219722749712716479147279517914791961791467
8919819819519195457357573579459185195569828964549592967124791247
2792579547526197517925113547925726675276256721792347251254259769253
6579525472567425251756626542656725615425674272562654725646746547
3425382567257259647542596735654594764695326526689478678474536339
3617174514567374567265157671642715757259215475757675154659457975
4932897985527427594628954719847897941789441774748974498347984198
7895794794789647898419479287689745907468794389745891459625737892475
7897814457918961477474759347369459892478747248474817489498648740894
4543641464485444674889977877798679445474664594877349749757574598
4599295697954905660851949458455143624236715595625474689457797474645
5795974924925245564452345584533285615851260645987869864376462666653
1357121256718299848948974594727974146376241554776779189414734747897
3892478947748474817485484648748954594646543644146448544467488997787
9445347464459482349743757937489874479844599295697954905660859494947
6634236256549492547692457972474584795975795924924974524598445234558
6155317668459828698642764426865345659848975145123131498156156565115
4962395498561945874895674978345648346455616319464867984577568797879
7152614261974656159665659647415519523428345514823486247627424472776
3671426145767756725452637573687729727295473425472453543543234434244
5215252354406762762472729148619182482225472655987342099947595454
3776143756748778277823177867156345915597653457631452456463274723423
7181756517567145656134567146556712551567156796595676559562345656657
9567255456794840654475652656457456594735465546561346453924571235
9577894978947459745718467659478569435713231562241723134375134634523
8745948948964934698736896434964896874528974987494491539819451989617
8716759191893457357457367712342245335782756235467457373881232777
5474644594827347437515374894476368744798445997956979549054608594947
3466247362565494925476924579724745847959757959249749752459844523457
8155353126684598286986427644268653456545313287121756718299848948974
4146517678415547767477596456776225123776143756748778277823178944177
9854798419894792957478937947937896478984194797874987459874489743895
4896743789747178979947897814458709898283287181289487124749718198819
4676493623236167678383262691761313473793966569634567994538924789475
1748548464874895489464494364146448544467488977877798679445474645
4974375753748987447984459929569795490566085949494596351466247236256
5475924579724745847959757959249249252459844523455845832856155312664
6986427644268653456598489751451231314981561565651154944564942395454
8748956749225345648346455616513464867984577568797895649861713261426
1596656596474155195234283455148234862476274244727653575753671426145
7254526375736877297272954734254724535434354323443234224772525215252
7624727291486191824822254726559873420999545593415552511595346596
1786578598798319819819345424739729731392733147629624721974629447
2964782964729907472969827456972159279795594975651954859179556745
9723797231295127961595179567927492394795296947295745791757597979